YOUR BRAIN WEIGHS 500 POUNDS

YOUR BRAIN WEIGHS 500 POUNDS

Change Your Mindset to Achieve Desired Outcomes

DERRICK R. PLEDGER

*Stay Tuned for More Mindset-Changing
Releases from the 500 Pound Series:*

500-Pound Strategies for Achieving Greatness

500-Pound Strategies for Climbing Any Ladder

LIONCREST
PUBLISHING

YOUR BRAIN WEIGHS 500 POUNDS
Change Your Mindset to Achieve Desired Outcomes

FIRST EDITION

ISBN   978-1-5445-4440-3 *Hardcover*
       978-1-5445-4439-7 *Paperback*
       978-1-5445-4441-0 *Ebook*

This book is dedicated to everyone who has failed at something in their lives. Failure does not define you. Your mind is the most daunting, most powerful, and most influential force on earth. You must feed it—nourish it with "nutrients" that drive productive habits, positive behaviors, and extreme focus.

CONTENTS

INTRODUCTION

When I was six years old, my YMCA camp counselor told my mother that I was "different" and repeatedly raved about how something was special about me. Whether it was true or not, I was naive enough to believe him. Turns out, I was not special; however, I have found a way to build a relationship with *achievement* that has changed the trajectory of my life. I wrote this book because I believe that I have a personal mandate to help you become the person you desire to be—the person who deep down you want to become.

I grew up in a single-parent household in Harrisburg, Pennsylvania. For years, my mother worked three jobs at once, so a hard-charging work ethic is in my DNA. I learned very early on that there is no hack to achieving your goals, no magic pill that melts off excess belly fat, no $59.95 course that will make you a real estate tycoon, and in most instances, no one is going to *give* you anything.

Just by choosing this book, you've demonstrated that there is some form of "greatness" you desire in your life and that you are willing to work for it. The entire purpose of this book is to help you understand the mindset, behaviors, and principles that will help you become the type of person who "achieves" every day.

I describe myself as an "Achievement Architect" because I've learned how behaviors and habits compound in a way that can drive you to meet your goals. As for my own achievements, here are a few:

1. At twenty-six years old, I received my first publishing deal (a book cowritten with Curtis "50 Cent" Jackson).
2. I was promoted to the rank of chief information officer of a Fortune 500 company by age forty.
3. A close friend and I built an export company (a "side hustle") that generated millions of dollars of revenue with zero inventory or an office.

Again, I am *not* special. I achieved these outcomes by following the principles and patterns you will read about in this book. Whether you are focused on climbing the corporate ladder, an entrepreneur aspiring to take your business to the next level, a person in need of another revenue stream to supplement your income, a creator seeking to make social impact, a real estate agent working to be a top salesperson, or an athlete looking for a winning edge, the lessons in this book will help you progress toward your goals. My life mission includes helping you achieve greatness according to your own definition.

This book is intended to be a "mindset manual" designed to challenge your perspectives, biases, and thoughts related to the process of achievement. You can flip to any page, read it in less than a minute, and return to your busy day. Every page has a lesson you can apply to your life. Think of it as a conversation between you and me, as well as a dialogue you can have with yourself.

First, I hope we can agree on a basic principle up front: our reality is being "manufactured" on a daily basis, which means our brains are on a constant diet of useless information—in other words, bullsh*t. We don't need to look far to assign blame: TV news, gossip sites, Facebook, LinkedIn, Instagram, TikTok, and on-demand streaming services that've made it possible to binge-watch our favorite shows.

Use your imagination for a moment. Can you envision your brain as if it were an actual body? Based on the excessive amount of time we spend ingesting unhealthy ideas, social media, and worthless content, our brains (as bodies) would appear morbidly obese. How much do you think your brain would weigh? Two hundred, three hundred, five hundred pounds?

The "diet" most of us feed our minds is pretty atrocious. Be honest with yourself. What does your brain's diet look like? Is it healthy? Balanced? Do you waste hours every day on social media or on activities that will neither add value to your life nor propel you to your goals? What is the last self-development book you read? Better yet, what was the last *book* you read, period? Do you watch the news every morning, Netflix throughout the day, and reality television in the evening? Studies show that most television shows and media have a negative spin; is that really what you want to feed your brain on a daily basis? Probably not.

Your brain is actually just like a body. In the same way that years of an unhealthy diet can result in diabetes, heart disease, or stroke, failing to prioritize learning, allowing negative thinking to dominate your mind, and ignoring discipline can cause your brain to become diseased also. The resulting conditions, such as stress, mental health issues, and endless procrastination will affect your behaviors and impede progress toward your goals.

I am not a self-help "guru." Merely reading this book will not change your life, make you rich, or solve your problems. But if you commit to the book's principles, it will transform your perspectives, overhaul your habits, and revolutionize the way you pursue your goals. I claim none of the ideas and lessons in this book (which I call "recipes") to be my own. They originate from a vast range of people—including some of the most successful people on earth down to my personal mentors and even a waitress I met in a diner. I compiled them over two years, during a period when I studied development content, conducted interviews, and journaled every single day as part of a campaign to make myself better. I've merged some of life's most valuable concepts into succinct, easy-to-read pages where you can glean a wealth of perspective and insight. Just as I completed a dedicated campaign of improvement, it is time for you to begin your own.

Now, let's begin your new "brain diet." I hope you've brought your appetite.

RECIPE #1: EMBRACE YOUR AMBITION

Ambition Drives Positive Change

Imagine a world without entrepreneurs, engineers, scientists, and thought leaders. Without them, there would be no cures for sickness or disease, no electric cars, none of the handheld computers we depend on every day (cell phones), and we most certainly would not have sent the *Spirit* rover to Mars. The best entrepreneurs, engineers, scientists, and thought leaders are extremely ambitious. Yet the word "ambition" can have a negative connotation.

For decades, we've allowed our culture—knowingly or unknowingly—to characterize ambition as negative, often seeing it associated with individualistic or self-serving perspectives. The reality is that ambition is one of the greatest drivers of positive change for humanity on Earth. It's time to change the narrative. Your ambitions are not selfish or vain—they are positive and, most times, a force for good. Embrace your ambitions and make a commitment to drive toward the outcomes you desire. Be ambitious, and don't get sidetracked by anyone who criticizes your aspiration to achieve greatness.

RECIPE #2: PRACTICE SELF-AWARENESS

Self-Awareness Is One of the Keys to Success

Have you ever been in a meeting or group dialogue where someone makes it his or her business to let everyone know they are the smartest person in the room? Interestingly, these individuals are rarely the ones with real authority within a group, but nonetheless, feel they have the right to commandeer the conversation. This behavior is the *worst* kind of self-sabotage because it not only shows a person's lack of self-awareness, but also their lack of emotional and social intelligence. The reason this matters is that emotional and social intelligence are two of the key factors that shape and determine our level of success.

I have a savvy colleague whom I will refer to as "Shawn." He's a great engineer who was a rising star and full of potential. But when one of his peers earned a well-deserved promotion, Shawn began to air his grievances in meetings. He could not understand how this particular person had been promoted before he was. He took the matter as a personal slight, which damaged his reputation. Be honest with yourself—are you one of those people who lacks self-awareness? If so, your journey to success will improve as soon as you start to change your behavior.

RECIPE #3: DEFINE GREATNESS

Don't Cheat Yourself Out of the
Possibility of Greatness

Greatness is defined as the "quality or state of being great or distinguished." Have you ever written down how greatness—per your own definition—will manifest itself in your own life? What would you need to do or accomplish to feel as if you had achieved greatness? What version of you would you consider great? If you cannot easily answer these questions, achieving greatness is virtually impossible.

Write down what greatness would look like within your family, your career, your financial life, your physical life, and your emotional life. You must be intentional and very clear about what greatness means to you. Otherwise, you are not only robbing yourself of the possibility of achieving your goals, but also robbing others who could benefit from your creativity, effort, service, or contribution to humanity. Capture your "greatness" vision, create a plan to pursue it, and commit yourself to executing on your plan.

RECIPE #4: WORTHWHILE PURSUITS

Pursuits That Are Worth Time and
Effort Will Demand an Uphill Climb

Since the time we played in sandboxes as children, we have been taught that hard work is the key to success. Most of us agree with this statement, but there is a missing piece to the "hard work = success" equation. We know there are millions of people who have worked hard every day of their lives but still struggled and never achieved the success they sought. What is missing for such people is a clear and compelling vision of what they are pursuing. Without a worthwhile pursuit or a clear outcome you are working toward, your time and effort will never be enough.

The truth is that most of us fail to come up with a worthwhile pursuit that will drive us to get off of the couch. Your objective should not be arbitrarily focused on being rich, successful, famous, or the best in your profession—success cannot be "wished" into existence. You must be very clear with yourself about what will make you get up early, skip meals, and sacrifice leisure and comfort. A worthwhile pursuit will drive you forward.

RECIPE #5: CHOOSE ACCOUNTABILITY

Weakness, Negativity, and Laziness
Do Not Get a Vote

Just as time, effort, and worthwhile pursuits are interconnected, the same goes for weakness, negativity, and laziness. If these three words were human, they'd probably be siblings because they are "born" from the same parents. There is a popular expression—"success leaves clues"—and there are published articles, including industry research (e.g., *Forbes* magazine and *Harvard Business Review*), that describe the habits and routines successful individuals follow. None include weakness, negativity, or laziness.

Of course, there is no one-size-fits-all approach, but the common themes are staying disciplined, waking up early, writing down your goals, and being intentional with your actions. This tried-and-true method is free. Nevertheless, why is it that most people ignore these proven success patterns? The answer is that we often fail to hold ourselves accountable. We make excuses, and we allow our minds to *choose* to let weakness, negativity, and laziness have a vote in our lives. That's right—it's a choice but it surely doesn't have to be. Your mind is not a democracy. Take charge of it.

RECIPE #6: IGNORE THE NOISE

Do Not Allow Others to Define You

The innate "power" that makes us human and separates us from animals is our ability to reason. Despite that, we often fail to use this power and listen too closely to the opinions, judgments, and advice of others. How many times have you heard someone say that "money is the root of evil," or that "starting a business is too risky," or "if it were me, I wouldn't do that."

The beauty of being an individual is that there is no law that says you must listen to other people—and yes, that means parents and family members, too. Of course, talking to those who have more wisdom and experience is always a good idea; there is value that can be gleaned from such conversations. Nevertheless, only *you* get to decide who you want to be. *You* decide what your goals are and what actions you will take to achieve them. Anything that runs counter to the vision you have for yourself is just "noise."

RECIPE #7: EVERY SECOND COUNTS

Time Is Precious—Don't Waste It

The great thing about time is that we all have the same amount of it no matter our race, religion, location, political affiliation, or gender. There are 86,400 seconds in a day. Let's break this down a bit. Most of us typically sleep for about 28,800 seconds, which translates into eight hours. Similarly, if we have a traditional nine-to-five job, we usually work for another 28,800 seconds. That means we have another 28,800 seconds for everything else. Okay, let's just cut that in half because many of us have children or parents to take care of on top of other priorities.

That leaves us with 14,400 seconds (four hours). Do you use this time to watch TV or scroll up and down social media pages? Or do you use this time to learn, go to seminars, build your credentials, or complete assignments that will help you move toward bigger and broader goals? Those who make the deliberate choice to invest in themselves will go beyond others who waste their free time. Pay attention to every second...they all count.

RECIPE #8: LOOK IN THE MIRROR

Lying to Ourselves Is Pointless

For many years, I looked at myself in the mirror but did not *really* see myself. I know that sounds nonsensical, but bear with me. For many of us, looking in the mirror is simply part of the morning routine. If you shift your mindset, something profound can result.

What I learned is that a mirror is inherently designed to make us accountable for our actions. I taught myself to use the mirror as a tool to keep me honest about my behaviors—both good and bad. For example, every day I look at myself and ask, "Did you give your best today?" I feel a sense of accomplishment when I can answer that I *did* give my best, regardless of the outcome I was driving toward. And there are other days when I know the answer is that I took shortcuts or chose comfort instead of facing a difficult task.

I can tell you from experience that lying to yourself is pointless. Your conscience knows when you did not give your best effort, whether it's work, school, or anything else. From this point forward, face the mirror daily and ask yourself the question. If you do not like the answer, be intentional and attack the day.

RECIPE #9: EMBRACE ADVERSITY

How Will You Respond When Bad Things Happen?

Sylvester Stallone's character in the *Rocky* film series is one of the most beloved movie roles of all time. My favorite is *Rocky IV*, as it blends an "underdog" storyline with that of two super-powers—the United States and Russia—going head-to-head on the world stage. The story ends with Rocky winning the fight, as well as the adulation of a mostly Russian crowd. We are all seeking a similar form of adoration and success in life. Never-theless, it is easy to forget how many times Rocky was knocked down during the fight with his opponent, Drago (played by Dolph Lundgren).

The punishment was brutal, but Rocky just kept coming back round after round. The most memorable part for me is when Rocky begins to turn the tide in the fight, and his cornerman passionately says, "You see—he's not a machine, he's a man!" In due course, Rocky gradually breaks Drago's spirit because he just keeps punching after he's knocked down repeatedly. These scenes are identical to our lives in many ways. You will be knocked down many times in life, but those who keep fighting, those who embrace adversity and learn from it, will end up victorious. Run toward adversity—not away from it.

RECIPE #10: BE READY TO GRIND

Knock on Doors Every Single Day

Can you imagine if a salesman came knocking on your door, trying to sell you a twenty-five-pound box of encyclopedias? Probably not, because most of us did not live in the golden age of the door-to-door salesperson. In the 1950s and 60s, however, door-to-door salesmen were commonplace.

In those days, the average door-to-door encyclopedia salesman lasted approximately three days before he quit (in all honesty, I would have lasted even less)—it took an average of one hundred "door knocks" to sell one set of encyclopedias. Yet there were generations of Americans who made a living and raised families in this line of work. So I've asked myself: what made these hard-working individuals different? The answer is something we all can learn from: they knew how to "grind." To them, there was no difference between the weekdays and the weekends. In fact, the weekends were better because that's when a door-to-door salesman was most likely to find people at home! Be ready to grind no matter what day of the week it is.

RECIPE #11: TRANSCEND YOUR FLAWS

When You Must, Give Yourself Some Latitude

In contemporary culture, the story of how a hero or heroine overcomes their flaws to save the day is found in many books, movies, and television shows. The storyline never gets old, even though we've seen it time and time again. We love a story of resilience in the face of adversity. The experiment that we call America is representative of the same concept. Despite all of our social ills, including racial and income inequality, I still maintain that we live in the greatest country on earth. Most of us believe the same thing, and—even though we know that America is always in pursuit of a more perfect union—we give our country a "break" when it comes to rendering judgment on it. We allow some wiggle room for the imperfections.

The question becomes: why do we fail to give ourselves the same latitude? We are all flawed beings who can be smarter, more attractive, a better entrepreneur, a better parent...the list goes on and on. Transcendence is *not* about being perfect—it is about recognizing you have flaws, about making a commitment to address those that are most detrimental to your life, and then continuing your pursuit to design a more perfect you.

RECIPE #12: MAKE A MAP

A Journey without Directions Leads Nowhere

If I had a dime for each time I've heard about the importance of goal setting, I'd be rich enough to pay each of you a thousand dollars to read this book. We all recognize that we need to establish well-articulated goals to achieve desired outcomes in our lives. Where most people fail is that just having goals is not enough. Imagine if you had a simple goal to drive from New York City to Washington, DC. If you haven't driven this route before, you know you will never make it without a map or GPS. It is not enough to simply know where you want to end up; you have to know how to get there.

This is an oversimplification, but you get the point. The analogy is this: becoming the person you want to be takes more than writing down a single goal or saying a single affirmation. You must plan each of the actions needed to meet your goal. You must learn to imagine the steps you will need to take to reach your objectives. This process takes time and forethought, but you will not reach your destination without it. Without a clear map, your goals are simply dreams that you wrote on a piece of paper.

RECIPE #13: SUCCESS MODELING

There's Nothing Wrong with Being a
Copycat When It Comes to Success

I have learned countless lessons from Tony Robbins, but one of his concepts, in particular, has had the greatest impact on me. He teaches that we need to practice *modeling* (I call it "success modeling"). The idea is this: while it is critical that we chart our own paths, we can learn a great deal from the success of others. We can model our paths after those who have achieved similar goals.

For me, success modeling provided an irreplaceable shortcut. At the new-hire orientation that I attended during my first week working for a defense contractor, I briefly met the chief information officer (CIO). At the time, I wasn't sure what a CIO actually did, but I could see enough to know that it was an important role. Over the next decade, I read everything I could about the skills, abilities, and experience that a great technology leader needs. Through books and in real life, I studied the journeys of many leading technology disruptors. Thirteen years later, I became a CIO. I am living proof that success modeling works.

RECIPE #14: INCREASE YOUR EFFICIENCY

Being Busy Is Not the Same as Being Productive

Have you ever said to yourself, "I'm busy all the time, but I don't feel like I'm getting anything done"? You're not alone, my friend. Even people who have achieved great success experience this moment of frustration and cognitive dissonance. But there's a way out of it, and that is developing systems that increase your efficiency and influence you to either do something or—better yet—to not do something.

Think of it this way: how much time do you spend in meetings every week? Are the meetings worth the time? After the meetings have ended, are there clear and defined actions that team members need to take? A simple hack to this, I have learned, is to challenge everyone who is present at a meeting to articulate the specific actions they will be taking following the meeting, and to name the time that activity will be completed. Asking everyone to be clear and accountable is a simple way to increase efficiency and can reduce scope creep or wasted time by orders of magnitude. If you don't believe me, try it for thirty days.

RECIPE #15: WELCOME CRITICISM

Criticism Helps You Confront Your Deficiencies

Even when we put a bit of lipstick on the word "criticism" and call it "constructive criticism," it still remains an emotionally charged phrase for most people. But criticism, whether we call it constructive or not, is a way that we learn to address our deficiencies.

Personally, I appreciate taking in all types of criticism, as it affords me the opportunity to think about my behaviors and to break through any impediments toward progress. Criticism is simply a mechanism designed to confront a deficiency. Welcome it instead of allowing your emotions to block your growth.

RECIPE #16:
BEAST MODE

Don't Sideline Your Inner Beast

If you are a sports fan, you're probably familiar with the phrase "beast mode." For those who are unfamiliar with this expression, it refers to when an athlete switches into high gear and performs at a very high level for a sustained period of time. I use the phrase at home with my two children who play sports, but I also use it within the context of academics (in my house, straight As are the standard).

I know that scoring high marks in the American education system is not a barometer of future success, but we live in a system where you must clear certain hurdles to be taken seriously (think SAT scores to get into elite colleges). I like the concept of beast mode because it codifies our ability to elevate our performance to achieve a desired objective. Many people, however, have settled on the idea that elevated performance happens only within a "finite" time period (a.k.a. the "mode"). To the best of your ability, be a "beast" twenty-four hours per day, seven days per week. Do not accept the idea that you must be in a "mode" to elevate your performance—your performance should *always* be elevated to achieve *big* goals.

RECIPE #17: FAILURE IS A TEACHER

Growth Is a Gift Hidden in Failure

Failure is uncomfortable. But if you're going to reach any of the meaningful goals you've set for yourself, then you need to change your perspective about failing or underperforming. We've all heard stories about Thomas Edison (failed thousands of times in his effort to invent the light bulb) or Michael Jordan (cut from his high school basketball team but went on to become arguably the greatest basketball player to ever live). In both cases, failure was a contributing factor to ultimate success.

You can think of failure as one of your most valuable teachers, even if it never says a word. Failure forces you to reevaluate the path or approach you are using to reach an outcome—and this is growth. Failure teaches you to recognize your shortfalls and avoid them in the future. When you try something and fail, you are "stretching" your ability to achieve an outcome. The most successful people in the world are also the best at failing—this may sound counterintuitive, but it's not. Fail hard and fail fast every single day and you'll grow exponentially.

RECIPE #18: PERSONAL CULTURE

Bad Culture Leads to Even Worse Outcomes

As Peter Drucker once famously said, "Culture eats strategy for breakfast." This doesn't mean we should abandon strategy, but it does make clear that a misaligned corporate culture can doom the most thoughtful and well-crafted strategies.

So why do so many companies fail to create a strong company culture? I don't have the answer, but I'll offer an analogy we can apply at the individual level—because, within ourselves, we all have our own cultures we build and enact. If you develop a set of weekly goals and devise a plan to achieve them but overdrink one night and lose three days of productivity, your culture of alcohol overconsumption has clearly compromised your strategy. The culture has defeated the strategy. The point is this: the personal culture you enact with yourself is just as important as the outcomes you are pursuing. Bad personal culture will ultimately impede progress toward your goals.

RECIPE #19: YOUR NETWORK IS GOLD

People Rarely Outgrow Their Social Circles

I've learned that if you socialize with "dumb people," chances are that either you are dumb yourself or you will be soon. This notion is so simplistic, yet many of us choose to surround ourselves with mediocrity. Why is that? Some research shows there is comfort in being unchallenged or having a feeling of superiority in a particular social group.

Consider the peers and professional circles you associate with. Do these individuals challenge you? Are you gaining value from the conversations you have with them? Do you discuss goals, creativity, or concepts that give you an edge? Or is the subject matter related to who won last night's football game, how much you hate your job, or your spouse's or partner's shortcomings? The hard truth is that it will be very difficult for you to become more successful than those in your close networks, because the ideas, goals (or lack thereof), and habits are typically shared across your social circles. Take a moment to assess your personal and professional networks. Do you need to make any changes to your associations? If so, start today.

RECIPE #20: PUSHING YOURSELF

There Is Immense Power in One More

In an earlier Recipe, we discussed how every single second counts. Now let's take this construct one step further. In life, we are constantly pursuing superiority—in our minds, in our health, and in our professions. So in our effort to achieve desired outcomes, why not push ourselves harder? For example, why not push yourself to go one extra minute on the treadmill every time you work out? Why not read over one more chapter as you prepare for an important exam or certification?

Every time you decide to complete one more—no matter the task—your life will begin to benefit from a compounding effect in which the "extra" effort will make you physically, mentally, and professionally superior to the person you were the day before. It will make you better equipped to tackle everyday tasks. It will reinforce habits that help you move toward your objectives. The power is in disciplining yourself to go for one more instead of settling for less than what you're capable of.

RECIPE #21: OVERCOMING UNCERTAINTY

Self-Doubt Is a "Dream Killer"

Having doubts about ourselves is normal. Self-doubt can come about for a variety of reasons, including childhood trauma, feelings of "not being good enough," or subscribing to the judgments of others. I've found there are strategies you can practice to prevent self-doubt from destabilizing progress. The first step is to give yourself a break—try to recognize what is driving your feelings of doubt. In many cases, these emotions stem from uncertainty, comparing ourselves to others, or allowing past experiences to define our future selves.

News flash! You are *not* your past. Understand that mistakes you've made in the past are not the enemy; confront them and use them to your advantage. Remember that you are always your harshest critic; be mindful of the thoughts you have about yourself. Use the power of positive thinking—meaning if you have a debilitating thought, counter it by training yourself to practice self-gratitude. Write down or recite five positive achievements you've completed at the end of every month. Self-care is the key to overcoming your internal doubts.

RECIPE #22: BE PREPARED

Leaders Are Proactive; Followers React

During my time as an undergraduate student at Virginia Tech, a mentor of mine introduced me to one of the most valuable concepts I've learned in my life. It was a phase referred to as the nine Ps: "Poor Preparation Promotes Poor Performance; Poor Performance Promotes Pain." I can tell you from experience that this principle is unquestionably true.

The most successful leaders, entrepreneurs, athletes, and scientists are always meticulously prepared. These kinds of people are constantly going on offense; instead of allowing things to "happen" to them, they create the conditions that lead to success. On the flip side, the individual who is unprepared will always be reacting to conditions or circumstances rather than controlling them. It's very simple—no one has ever been harmed by overpreparation. Make it a habit.

RECIPE #23: ELEVATE YOUR ENERGY LEVEL

Low Energy Is a Productivity Killer

Take a moment to remember the excitement you expressed as a kid when you discussed what you wanted to be in the future. Whether it was a police officer, astronaut, architect, or professional athlete, it was pure joy to fantasize about what your life would be like once you realized your dream. Then what happens? Life has a way of putting roadblocks, impediments, and adversity in your way. Consequently, we lose some of our drive and motivation as we begin to navigate challenges.

What you must understand is that our energy, which is defined as "the capacity or power to work," is totally within our control. Energy is a by-product of our diet, exercise regimen, and the time we spend developing our minds. The problem many of us have is a misalignment between our energy capacity and the level of our dreams. Be honest with yourself—is your level of energy consistent with the level of the outcomes you desire? If it isn't, those outcomes will *never* be achieved. Commit to ensuring that your energy is high enough to propel you to your dreams. You can do this by controlling your habits, behaviors, and what you pay attention to every day.

RECIPE #24:
REAL EFFORT

You Can't Want 100 Percent When
You Only Give 80 Percent

A close relative to *energy* is *effort*. You can be extremely ener-
getic and decide to wake up at 5:00 a.m. to go to the gym or to
work on a project. But if you give "half-assed" effort, progress
on your goals will be elusive. Then there are those who exceed
the 100 percent effort level, and their results are quite different.
For extended periods of time, Elon Musk routinely worked one-
hundred-hour weeks. He has earned his status as the richest
individual in the world (as I am writing this, his net worth is
$261 billion).

I am not saying you need to begin working hundred-hour weeks.
But I am saying you need to be conscious of the effort you
apply daily. This translates to every aspect of your life, including work, relationships, exercise, school, business, and your
health. Demonstrating a lack of effort can be devastating and
will compromise your ability to reach your goals. Don't trick
yourself into believing that you'll reach your goals if you give
anything less than 100 percent.

RECIPE #25: FACE YOUR FEARS

*Fear Is a Tiny Evil That Eats
Us from the Inside Out*

When I discovered that fear is a phenomenon that our mind essentially manufactures, it was incredibly liberating. I am not referring to the instinctual fear you'd have if a bear was chasing you in the woods. I am talking about the type of fear that prevents us from taking specific actions to reach the outcomes we desire.

Some of us have a fear of failure, competition, judgment, or inadequacy; others fear being challenged or simply being uncomfortable. But most of these fears are illusory—they are tricks that our minds play on us. The good news for you is there are no bears stopping you from launching a business, rehearsing a presentation twenty times, or making fifty more sales calls to close a deal. When you face life head-on and climb to the other side of fear, you will be amazed at the feelings of accomplishment you will experience. There are no bears chasing you. Face your fear, and take decisive action.

RECIPE #26: SELF-CONTROL GOES A LONG WAY

Common Vices Will Derail Your Pursuits

During my college days, I was a fan of the "work hard, play hard" mantra. However, sometimes the *play hard* side of things resulted in regrets. For instance, there were times when I'd socialize well into the early hours of Sunday morning, leaving myself unable to use Sunday evening to prepare for Monday's priorities. Some of you know that a "hangover" rarely leads to notable accomplishments. Overindulging in alcohol may not be an issue for you specifically, but life's "vices" come in many shapes and sizes (e.g., shopping, drugs, social media, television, and nightlife). We all have them.

What's important is to be honest about your transgressions so you can develop controls that prevent your priorities from being derailed. For example, if you tend to overspend, maybe you should leave the charge cards at home and only carry the amount of cash you are able to spend. Common-sense self-control mechanisms can go a long way. Use them.

RECIPE #27: THE TRUTH ABOUT BALANCE

There Is No Such Thing as "Work–Life Balance"

I have a love–hate relationship with weekends. Like everyone else, I look forward to Friday night. But in reality, I typically think of the weekend as just another two workdays at the end of the week. This orientation toward Saturdays and Sundays has served me well in my life journey.

The weekends aren't for leisure in my opinion—not if you are seriously committed to reaching your professional, entrepreneurial, or personal goals. When you are enjoying a movie, a leisurely drive across the country, or a night out on the town, your competition is grinding it out. I have nothing against taking some time to unwind, but making leisure a habit impacts productivity. The whole idea of work–life balance has been a fallacy since the phrase was conceived. If you aim to be a high performer at anything, there is no such thing as work–life balance—not, at least, in the way many people talk about it. There are no days off on the journey to success.

RECIPE #28: WHAT MAKES A CHAMPION?

You Can't Win without Momentum

Many of us believe that people who are performing at the highest level—whether in sport or industry—have some sort of secret. Sorry, my friend, this idea is false. Champions do not have a secret or special type of edge over others. They are the people who are willing to go to work. When they are tired, they go to work. When they are sick, they go to work. When they perform terribly, they go to work. When they lose, or fail, they go to work. When adversity blocks them from success, they go to work.

Whatever the roadblock is, it does not matter—champions just keep going to work. As a result of their discipline, they build momentum, and once they have it, it's hard to stop them. Countless successful athletes, entrepreneurs, and other professionals will tell you this. If you need examples of folks who made *going to work* a lifestyle, you can start here: Tom Brady, Michael Jordan, Sara Blakely, Bill Gates, Serena Williams, Mark Cuban, Jay-Z, Grant Cardone, Jocko Willink, Joe Rogan, Oprah, Warren Buffett, Andy Frisella, Alex Hormozi, Dwayne Johnson... and I could go on and on.

RECIPE #29: IMAGINATION IS POWER

"Imagination Is More Important than Knowledge"

The above quote, credited to Albert Einstein, may seem counterintuitive. Yet, when you unpack his words, you can see his point. It is easy to take the technology and physical structures we are surrounded by for granted as we go about our busy lives. But all of that infrastructure began as a thought in someone's mind. Without the imagination of such people, there would be no trains, automobiles, mobile phones, vaccines, robots, theme parks, or skyscrapers. This list could fill the rest of this book!

Imagination, more than knowledge, allows us to change the game that humanity is always playing. It enables us to make our lives better, confront social problems, and address the needs of humanity. Take an hour and use your imagination to envision the life you really want to live. Think about it, then will yourself to believe in your vision, and start taking concrete action to move toward it.

RECIPE #30: YOUR SUCCESS IS NOT ABOUT YOU

Success Demands That We Serve Others

We live in a world driven by self-image and self-centeredness. Social media is full of individuals posting about where they are, what they are wearing, or how much money they have made (or blown). It must be quite tiresome to have to inform the world of your every move, every fifteen minutes. I am actually glad we have so many people engaging in this silly behavior because, for me, it means fewer people that you and I have to compete with on our journey to success.

The interesting thing about success is that it's not really about YOU. The most prosperous entrepreneurs, leaders, and athletes find ways to solve problems or serve others. Professional athletes get chastised for their exorbitant salaries. They bring joy, however, to millions of spectators—and this is a form of service. Jeff Bezos revolutionized order fulfillment on a global scale and made it possible for people to order pretty much anything from the comfort of their home. That is yet another form of service. The equation is simple: the more people you serve, the more successful you will be.

RECIPE #31: STICK TO "PLAN A"

Don't Fall Victim to "Plan B"

We all know Arnold Schwarzenegger from his famous roles in the *Conan the Barbarian* and *Terminator* movies. However, many are not aware of his inspiring journey from the farms of Austria to bodybuilding champion and Hollywood megastar. His story is one of true grit. During one of Arnold's speeches, he divulged a simple yet profound idea that runs counter to what we've all learned as children. He passionately conveyed that none of us should have a "Plan B."

We all create Plan Bs to fall back on if we don't achieve our primary goals. But for Arnold, the "Plan B effect" absolves us from being accountable to what we originally set out to do. The time we spend on creating Plan B should be allocated to furthering our commitment to reach Plan A. Do not give yourself an "out" or an escape valve when it comes to achieving your desired outcomes. The mere exercise of creating a Plan B subconsciously reinforces that you do not believe in yourself enough to reach Plan A. Devise your Plan A and stick to it.

RECIPE #32: BEWARE OF THE SNOOZE BUTTON

If You Hit the Snooze Button, You've Already Lost the Day

My morning alarm is set for 5:02 a.m. every day, including weekends. This may seem like a bizarre time; however, in my warped mind, allowing myself to sleep past 5:00 a.m. gives me a sense of counterfeit comfort. I know it makes no sense, and to be honest, there is nothing comfortable about waking up at this time every day.

So why do I do it? Why not just hit the snooze and turn over for another half hour of sleep? I have two reasons. First, I can hear fitness expert David Goggins saying, "Get up mother*(&@#%" in my mind. Secondly, I know there is someone else out there who is going to work. He or she is already winning the day, and I know that if I hit the snooze button, I am falling further behind. The discipline you develop by deciding not to hit the snooze button will begin to permeate into other areas of your life. When the alarm goes off, get up and make progress.

RECIPE #33: DON'T QUIT

There Is Nothing Good on the
Other Side of Quitting

From my perspective, quitting a pursuit because of adversity is one of the worst choices a human being can make. I am not talking about quitting smoking or exiting a failing relationship. I am referring to failing to execute on a plan you created to achieve a goal.

Quitting on your goals almost always leads to a deep sense of regret. Yes, sometimes we want to give up—we've all been there. We're human. However, I've found that if you honestly ask yourself about who you will be letting down if you quit, you will definitely be less prone to change your course. Remind yourself why you started your pursuit. Remember your original motivations. Remember the hunger you once had. Now, take a few minutes today and write down your "why." You'll be glad to have it to turn to in the moments when you feel like quitting.

RECIPE #34: DATA VERSUS FEELINGS

Make Data-Driven Decisions

Though we often use the words *feelings* and *emotions* interchangeably, their actual meanings are very different. Emotions are real sensations you feel in your body, while feelings are derived from thoughts in our minds.

Emotions are driven by the body's reaction to a present reality; feelings can be understood as our thoughts and perceptions that result from past experiences, fears, or even misplaced beliefs. This is a critical dynamic to understand because many of us make life decisions driven by feelings that are *not* aligned to current realities—we fall victim to our past, our fears, or inaccurate visions of the future. There is a way to counteract this condition, which is to ensure that accurate, up-to-date information drives every decision you make, whether it concerns your career, health, relationships, or future. Do your research. Use data instead of feelings to drive your life decisions.

RECIPE #35: BEWARE OF THE OPINION WEB

Free Yourself from Others' Judgments

Can you imagine if a spider built a web, ended up getting stuck in it, and then another spider came along and ate the first spider for lunch? This is exactly what we do to ourselves when we give too much credibility to other people's opinions. The "opinion web," as I call this, is responsible for the demise of many dreams. Opinion webs can influence us not to follow our dreams or dissuade us from taking a risk because someone said our idea was "stupid" or impossible.

Take a moment to remember Nelson Mandela's famous words: "Everything is impossible until someone does it." No person's opinions, perceptions, or actions can actually block you from moving toward your goals unless you allow it. As long as you have a plan and stick to it, the opinions of others do not matter, regardless of whether those opinions are good, bad, or indifferent. Don't let your opinion web result in your goals being "eaten."

RECIPE #36: ATTITUDE AND EFFORT

Attitude + Effort = Progress

Attitude and effort are two of the most important ingredients of success. Yet we do very little to teach children about either. At school, children learn about music, language, and the history of the Middle Ages, but there is no curriculum devoted to the value of a positive attitude or the importance of effort.

Increasingly, we leave adolescents to their own devices when it comes to these behaviors. Recent studies show that generational "work ethic" has decreased steadily. More and more, parents, coaches, and mentors play an incredibly important role in teaching children about the relationship between attitude and effort. When you add a good attitude to a solid effort, the overall result is usually noticeable progress toward a desired outcome. Take an inventory of how your attitude has affected your outcomes over the past year. Are you satisfied with the effort you expended to make progress?

.

RECIPE #37:
EMPATHY MATTERS

Build a Culture of Empowerment

According to psychologist Daniel Goleman, skills such as communication, social awareness, and motivation are just as important to an individual's ultimate success as their "intelligence." In fact, those who leverage social skills and empathy to galvanize a group or team usually achieve more success than those who don't. This applies to both family and the workplace and is fundamental in creating a culture where people are not afraid to express themselves. You should always welcome diversity of thought.

An empowerment culture is one that encourages people to bring their entire selves to work, where shared commitment drives behaviors instead of leading like a "drill sergeant." As an army veteran, I have nothing against drill sergeants. However, as a leader or individual contributor driving toward your goals, recognize that most people will not respond well when spoken to as if they are wearing a uniform. Use empathy instead.

RECIPE #38: EXPONENTIAL GROWTH

Maintain a Persistent Focus on Improving Yourself

Compound interest is one of the greatest inventions known to man. However, the sad reality is the vast majority of people either do not understand how it works or what its benefits are. All compound interest really means is that we have the opportunity to make money from the money we already have—a simple principle that has created many wealthy individuals. You can think of it as a "double whammy," as it results in exponential growth over time.

Maintaining a persistent focus on improving yourself carries the same benefit. It is no secret that the most successful people in the world are avid readers and see themselves as lifelong students. The more you learn, the more knowledge and depth you will have to draw upon to influence your decisions—decisions that will move you closer to your goals. When you dedicate yourself to habits that improve your physical, mental, or social faculties, the results will begin to compound in an exponential fashion.

RECIPE #39: PLAN YOUR SURROUNDINGS

Don't Sabotage Your Environment

I am willing to bet that many of you have a family room or living area where the furniture is oriented around a huge television. Yet we wonder where the time has gone after we've spent two hours after work glued to Netflix or Hulu. Or you've committed to sticking to the new diet, but you still have glazed donuts and a refrigerator full of leftover takeout. The amount of "environmental sabotage" that we apply to ourselves in our daily lives is astonishing. By environmental sabotage, I mean our willingness to surround ourselves with conditions that stand in the way of our goals, instead of conditions that promote our growth and development.

Obviously, the key here is to arrange your environment in a manner that helps you make the right choices. Do not allow yourself to experience rewards or leisure unless the prerequisite of hard work or effort has been satisfied. Shape your living and working environments so that they promote productivity—not procrastination and waste.

RECIPE #40: THERE IS NO CASUAL ROUTE TO SUCCESS

You Should Stop Being So "Casual"

When I need a "grind check," which is the process I use to prevent myself from getting too comfortable, I tune in to my good friend Ed Mylett. In reality, we are not actually friends and I've never met him, but I do consume a lot of his content on YouTube. In particular, he published a twelve-minute video that I've watched over one hundred times. Titled "You're Too Casual," the video shows Ed delivering a fiery speech that discusses how winners attack life and resist casual behaviors.

Most people wake up casually instead of getting up early to get after the day. They set casual goals. They have casual habits. They are casual at work and are satisfied to meet expectations rather than exceed them. They are casual about their health, as well as commitments to their families. Whatever dreams they may have in the back of their minds will never become a reality, because they've allowed *casualness* to become the norm. For the rest of us, however, their behavior means less competition to achieve our goals. Commit yourself to grinding every day, and leave casual behavior to underachievers. Don't be casual about anything in your life.

RECIPE #41: CHOOSE DISCOMFORT

Average Is the Close Relative of Comfort

Pittsburgh is hands down one of my favorite places to visit. It's almost like hard work is part of peoples' DNA there, regardless of their race, profession, gender, or religion. You may have heard of Mike Tomlin, the longtime head coach of the Pittsburgh Steelers. Tomlin is famous (or infamous) for his idea that discomfort is the pathway to personal growth. I couldn't agree more. I enjoy doing things that "suck," and you should too. When you stretch yourself—meaning that you deliberately face uncomfortable situations—your mind as well as your capacity to endure expands.

Discomfort builds your ability to exercise dominion over the defeatist thoughts that may happen in your head (e.g., *It's too hot to go for a run* or *I'm too tired to finish my project today*). The growth is in the struggle. Worthwhile outcomes often require confronting undesirable and difficult activities. Weak people seek comfort; you can do the opposite. Discomfort is a critical ingredient in your success journey.

RECIPE #42: LET YOUR PASSION PREVAIL

Don't Talk Yourself Out of Seeking Your Dreams

Second-guessing our actions is part of life. Whether you've kicked yourself for not going all out for a promotion, lacked the courage to ask someone on a date, or failed to launch a business idea, none of us is immune to being talked out of pursuing our goals by our own minds. I have talked myself out of taking risks on any number of occasions—that is, until I finally learned that taking risks can lead to great outcomes.

Safe, defeatist thinking rarely leads to success. If you are passionate about something, you must guard yourself against any negative self-talk that may compromise or derail your drive toward your objectives. You can do this by controlling your thoughts and the stories you tell yourself. Prevent debilitating thoughts from poisoning your decision-making processes. Control what you think about and let your passions lead the way.

RECIPE #43: MAKE MISTAKES EVERY DAY

*Play It Safe to Be "Good," or Take
Risks to Be "Great"*

Many of us have heard that it takes ten thousand hours of practical exercise and effort to become a subject matter expert in any field of study, trade, or profession. So why do we act surprised when we make mistakes along the way? Our school systems, the workplace, and even the sports world reinforce the idea—whether intentional or not—that we shouldn't make mistakes. The truth is that our mistakes can bring out the best in all of us.

I am willing to bet that the people journeying to becoming an expert in their field make many thousands of mistakes—small ones, medium ones, and large ones. Every mistake you are willing to confront head-on comes with an opportunity to grow and learn. Change your attitude about mistakes—if you aren't making any, you are simply playing it too safe.

RECIPE #44: YOUR HABITS AFFECT YOUR POCKETS

Your Financial Condition Is
Always a Reflection of You

As part of your "brain diet," I've stressed the importance of habits and how they compound to create our life experiences. Let's now look at habits from a different perspective—the financial dimension. Pick up your phone or computer and take a look at the balances in your bank account(s). If your balance exceeds $50,000, or even $100,000, good for you...you deserve credit. If you are frowning because your account is low, you deserve credit too—just the wrong kind of it.

Regardless of what number you see, it is a reflection of your financial habits. The number you see demonstrates that you value saving money, that you make impulse purchases, that you know how to invest, or that you are caught up in the latest fashion or automobile trends. When you change your habits related to money, your financial condition will change. Your total wealth is and always will be a reflection of your financial habits and attitude toward consumption.

RECIPE #45: MAGIC PILLS AREN'T REAL

Your Body Composition Is No Accident

Despite what the Instagram influencers tell you, there is no miracle pill or potion that is going to help you lose weight or transform your body. No matter how hard the influencers try, the formula for losing weight doesn't change: calories eaten minus calories burned over time. If you look in the mirror and don't like what you see—guess what, it's no one's fault but your own. If you like what you see, then fantastic! Either way, what you see is directly attributable to your own eating and exercise habits.

I've found that the key to sticking to a healthy eating regimen and staying consistent with exercise is to make sure you give yourself the right purpose and incentives. If you have children, wouldn't you want to live longer so you can play with your grandchildren? Having a terrible diet and poor exercise routine doesn't mean you won't play with them, but it reduces the probability you will. If you aspire for good health, you have to make sure your habits are aligned with your intentions. Your body is a living, breathing reflection of your own behaviors.

RECIPE #46: MAKE THE RIGHT FRIENDS

Seek Out People Who Are Better than You

Countless academic studies suggest that our peer groups are often accurate indicators of our future physical, mental, social, and financial conditions. We've all learned that you cannot pick your family members, but you can certainly select your friends, peers, and social circles. The feeling of inadequacy may lead us away from building relationships with those we perceive as "better" than us—more intelligent, more attractive, more successful, wealthier, etc. This is a serious problem because it prevents us from exploiting opportunities to learn from those who have achieved the outcomes we desire for ourselves.

If you want to be rich, you should make every effort to associate with wealthy people. If you want to be in shape, make friends with people who work out regularly. Think of it this way: are you more likely to keep going to the gym if you go alone or if you have peers who can keep you engaged and committed? The people you associate with, and the outcomes you desire, are intertwined.

RECIPE #47: MANAGE TASKS, LEAD PEOPLE

Management Is about Systems;
Leadership Is about People

John Wooden, the famed basketball coach, developed what is known as the "Pyramid of Success." The pyramid is a roadmap made up of twenty-five common behaviors—for example: cooperation, self-control, team spirit, and resourcefulness. Today, many people use the pyramid as a guide to drive individual success. But I believe Wooden would disagree that this is the pyramid's intent. He would say that it's about a system of leadership. Wooden didn't always have the best players, yet he built a coaching legacy like no other. How? His success was a direct result of his ability to motivate individuals with vastly different backgrounds and strengths to dedicate themselves to a common goal.

This is what real leadership is all about. Management is about structuring tasks and processes, and seeing that all the tasks required to achieve an outcome are assigned. But leadership is about people and ensuring that all members of a team are aligned with larger goals or objectives. People aspire to be led, not managed. Are you a leader or a manager?

RECIPE #48: ESCAPE THE RAT RACE

Diversify

We've all heard the phrase "rat race." It refers to the path that many people take in life: school, college, graduate school for some, and then a nine-to-five job for the next thirty or forty years until retirement. Along the way, you may change jobs, have a few life crises, and pay a significant swath of your income in taxes. But if you are determined to be really successful—uniquely successful—is this the right path? If we study the paths of thought leaders and Fortune 500 executives, we see that this is not necessarily the path they have taken. The problem with being in the rat race is that there is no diversification—your livelihood is totally dependent on one income stream. Most individuals who create wealth that can be passed on to future generations achieve this feat via entrepreneurship, invention, investments in hard assets, or by developing a diversified stock portfolio that compounds over time.

Of course, not everyone has a goal to create generational wealth; however, following the patterns that allow you to do so—even if on a small scale—will enable your family to have more options and access to whatever you desire. The lesson here is simple: *diversify*.

RECIPE #49: TALENT VERSUS SKILL

Talent Is Natural; Skill Is Made

Talent is free, but skill usually costs time, energy, and effort. *Talent* is the inherent aptitude to do something—we sometimes call this "a God-given ability." *Skill*, on the other hand, is developed through repetition, learning, and practice. Building the right skill explains why average people can become wildly successful in sports, business, and industry, but talented individuals often fail to live up to expectations when they rely on talent alone. Golfers like Tiger Woods or Jordan Spieth make what they do look so easy. Why? Because they are loaded with talent—we can only dream of playing at their level.

But talent alone is never enough, because anything we do, even if we're already good at it, can be improved by coaching, attention to detail, and building new skills. That's why Tiger and Jordan, despite their prodigious talent, spend countless hours practicing. It doesn't matter what your profession, industry, or passion is—to distinguish yourself from others, you must work every day to hone the skills that will drive you toward your desired outcomes.

RECIPE #50: HAPPINESS STARTS WITHIN

Control Your Responses to External Events

We sometimes think, *If I only had more money, I'd be less stressed and so much happier,* or *If they would give me more chances, I would be in a better place.* Looking to find happiness from other people, or from material goods, is usually a losing proposition. Furthermore, no life journey is uniformly happy. There will always be hardship and adversity, as well as victories and bliss. Dr. Sylvia Boorstein nails it in her book *Happiness Is an Inside Job,* when she says that how we respond to life's events forms the basis of our happiness. And guess what? You possess the ability to control how, when, and why you respond to events.

Bad things will happen to you; accept this as a fact and decide how you will react when things happen. You can't control everything that happens to you, but you can control the strategy you will use to protect your inner happiness. Stop letting external factors control your inner emotions.

RECIPE #51: LIVE FOR TODAY

Yesterday Is Gone and Tomorrow Is Not Promised

How many times have you kicked yourself for something that happened yesterday, or last week? We spend way too much time stressing over past events. And for no reason, because no matter how hard we try, we cannot go back in time and do things differently. The solution is putting what you've done in your "mistake box" and just leaving it for dead. Your mistake box is a critical tool you should add to your daily routine—not to remind you of everything you screwed up, but to give you reference material that can influence your behavior in the present and future.

A life hack that can encourage your progress is to wake up and write down the five main things that you want to accomplish that day. In effect, you are making a "contract" with yourself, and the act of writing down these items will influence your behavior through the course of the day. Imagine if you did this every day for one week; that translates into thirty-five critical things you will have completed. Yesterday is gone and tomorrow may never come—focus on making progress today.

RECIPE #52: THE LAZINESS TRAP

*If You Want to Fail to Reach Your
Goals, Laziness Can Help*

Oscar Wilde, the Irish poet, said, "Experience is the hardest kind of teacher. It gives you the test first and the lesson afterward." This is very profound. Inactivity—or, more bluntly, laziness—is the best friend of nonproductivity, because laziness produces *nothing*.

Activity propels us toward our desired outcomes. This is not rocket science. I am shocked, however, by how many people complain about not achieving an outcome or particular lifestyle but can't recognize—or don't care about—the impact of laziness. You cannot expect to reach your goals if your day-to-day behavior is in any way lazy.

RECIPE #53: BE A WINNER

Winners Persevere in Triumph and in Loss

We see a winner as the person or team that scores the most points or succeeds in a competition. But this definition is overly simplistic. In today's world, winners are *learners*. They are people who see risks and setbacks as opportunities to refine their approach to work, life, relationships, and wealth creation. In the face of adversity—and even when losing!—they maintain a mindset that prevents progress-killing self-doubt, procrastination, or fear of failure. So how do winners do this? It begins with a positive self-image and a core belief that things in their life are not happening to them, but that they are responsible for the results of their own behaviors. If they underperform on a task, they own it instead of blaming others or making excuses.

The key trait of a winner is that they are determined to reach their desired objectives—not because they are afraid of losing, but because they've embraced winning as one of their pursuits. The allure of winning is found in the perseverance and determination that keeps driving you, regardless of the losses you encounter on your way.

RECIPE #54: WHAT'S YOUR ENDGAME?

Start with Your Finish Line in Mind

Today, a trusted friend of mine argued that having goals just sets people up to fail. That runs counter to my own thinking, but I listened to his rationale. His presumption was that when one sets a goal and fails to achieve it, the failure can negatively impact self-esteem or an individual's feelings of self-worth. Maybe this is true for some people. But I believe that incremental goals allow you to create productive habits that build continuous momentum.

Even if you fail to meet a specific goal, your habits should persist because you are so focused on the "endgame." Your endgame is ultimately what you consider to be your best life or specific conditions that you'd like to create for yourself and those around you. You will stick to your habits because you care enough about the endgame not to let distractions derail your pursuit. Make sure your endgame is important enough to maintain your self-discipline and focus, despite the failures you will face along the way.

RECIPE #55: SUCCESS DOESN'T HAPPEN TO YOU

Don't Just Make Goals—Become the Person Who Will Achieve Them

There are thousands of books that promise to offer tricks or a formula that will ensure you achieve maximum success. Some books promote productivity fads, and others recite time-tested principles. But the truth is that every path to success is different—there is no prescription that works for everyone. What is true for every successful person, however, is that their success is a direct result of the person they become in pursuit of their dreams.

Success does not simply happen to you. It happens as a result of:

1. having the right mindset,
2. making both strategic and tactical plans for your life,
3. being disciplined and holding yourself accountable for sticking to your plan, and
4. surrounding yourself with individuals who are "pushers" or "ladders."

Pushers are family, friends, or associates who are aware of your goals and help you stay on course. Ladders are those who help create the conditions you need to reach your objectives. You do not *become* successful—you become a person whom success is *attracted* to.

RECIPE #56: INTENTIONAL CONVERSATIONS

Small Talk Is a Time Killer

Small talk is conversation that will not result in any new information or lead to an action to be completed in the future. There is nothing wrong with sharing pleasantries with a colleague, customers, or associates. Being respectful of an individual's time is what I refer to as *conversational courtesy*. This is an important concept to understand because we know that most high-performing people have a specific goal or intent in mind when engaging in conversation.

We too can know what our objectives are and employ active listening to understand the objectives of those we are speaking with. Putting this into practice will help you drive toward specific outcomes more efficiently, and with a better understanding of the actions that your desired outcome will require. Make it a priority to know exactly what you want to gain out of every conversation you participate in.

RECIPE #57:
OUTCOME ETHIC

*You Can't Have a Million-Dollar Dream
with a Thousand-Dollar Work Ethic*

Daymond John is a founder of the FUBU clothing line—you may know him from the hit TV show *Shark Tank*. What many people don't know is that John spent several years working as a waiter while he and his partners bootstrapped FUBU. John's days of waiting tables ended prior to FUBU's transformation into a $350-million per-year enterprise, but whether as a waiter or an entrepreneur, he always had a tremendous work ethic, and one that was not impacted by either failure or missteps.

"Work ethic" does not simply mean "working hard." It means that you are focused on an activity that results in a worthy reward or outcome. Your work ethic should be aimed at creating the capacity to produce outcomes in a timely and efficient manner, such that you can devote more time to higher-value activities. Worthy outcomes only occur when your capacity to produce results is aligned with what it takes to achieve a specific goal. To build more capacity, you must work harder because there are only twenty-four hours in a day.

RECIPE #58: SET GOOD TRAPS

Good Mousetraps Start with Tasty Cheese

Imagine that you are a mouse on the hunt for a meal and you come across three mousetraps. The trap on the left contains old, moldy cheese. The trap in the middle contains powdered cheese. And the trap on the right contains chef-inspired, gourmet cheese cuts. Which one would you pick? In our lives, we confront (and create) choices like these every day. Whether you are attempting to win an argument or to achieve consensus within a group, you must learn how to appeal to people's emotions as well as recognize what motivates them.

The most dominant levers driving human behavior are *fear* and *pleasure*. You can use fear as a mechanism to persuade action—an example of this is the millions of home security systems that are sold every year (even though the chances of a home invasion are relatively slim). The pleasure lever is simple—if you understand what pleases someone, align your desired outcome with activities that bring them joy or accomplishment. Going forward, set "tasty" traps to drive influence and action.

RECIPE #59: BE WARY OF "FAVORS"

Use Good Judgment When Considering Reciprocity

Has someone ever done something nice for you, and you found it hard to return the favor in a meaningful way? Did you feel a sense of guilt or shame? If you did, it's because we are conditioned to feel a sense of "psychological debt," which means that if someone does us a favor, we feel an obligation to give something in return.

Research shows that people like to return favors. The theory that describes this phenomenon is the *rule of reciprocation*. While this principle has served humanity well, there is a danger in blindly returning every favor. There are certain people, groups, and countries that deliberately abuse these rules in order to appeal to their own self-interest. Before you return any favor, you should perform an honest assessment of the purported intent of the party who did a favor for you. Ask yourself if it is genuine or if there is an ulterior motive. Not every "favor" is worth returning.

RECIPE #60: MAKE GOOD HABITS A "HABIT"

Sticking to a Routine Is Critical

There are multiple schools of thought about routines and their impact on success and achievement. In my view, routines are simply a series of habits that an individual sticks to, perhaps in the belief that sticking to the routine will pay dividends over time. If you work out every day for ninety days, it is probable that you will be in better shape after three months.

James Clear's book *Atomic Habits* taught me something very important: that habits are not sustainable unless you create an environment that enables you to stick to them. Routines are similar to habits in that you cannot achieve excellence in anything you do without a regimen of actions that compound over time. Your professional and social environments must be conducive to the routines you have committed to.

RECIPE #61: LOSING IS A CHOICE

It Takes Effort to Be a Loser

In today's political and social climate, it is difficult to find areas of common ground. Nevertheless, I am quite sure that everyone—regardless of race, religion, or nationality—would agree that no one wants to be called a "loser." Being categorized as a loser—in any way, shape, or form—is bad. In the business world—if not life in general—how much of a loser you are comes down to how willing you are to be prepared.

Winners are those who meticulously prepare and take deliberate action to organize their activities in a manner that gives them the best chance of being successful. Alternatively, losers make the choice *not* to prepare; thus, their performance exposes their lack of initiative, discipline, or attention to detail. In this regard, we could say that being a loser is a choice. For example, if you had an important presentation to give and decided to wait until the night before to prepare, then you made a choice not to set yourself up for success. The way you used the time you allocated to other activities, rather than the preparation of the presentation, was within your control. This same concept applies to practically every facet of your life. Don't make the choice to be a loser.

RECIPE #62: FIND THE COURAGE TO THINK BIG

True Passion Is Never Found in Small Things

What does it take to change the world? I will offer that life-changing technologies, inventions, or solutions to immense challenges always begin with a pioneer who had the passion to dream *big*. Why is it, then, that so many people dream so small? The answer to that question lies in how our minds work. The mind is designed to do two things: keep our bodily functions running and protect us from danger. That said, we must be very intentional about choosing to be courageous in the face of danger.

One of the most effective tools that the mind uses to influence our behavior is *fear*. And this is why so many of us fail to create big, bold visions. Any big vision is going to come with a chance of failure—and probably a relatively high one. So we choose to play it safe instead of giving our own passions a shot. It requires courage to develop a lofty vision. It takes true passion and determination to actually achieve it. You must become fully immersed in your vision to maintain your passion through the adversity and failures you will experience along the way. Think *big*—the bigger the vision, the greater the chance of changing the world.

RECIPE #63: FORTY HOURS IS NOT ENOUGH

There Are Never Any Traffic Jams
When You Go the Extra Mile

The idea of a forty-hour workweek is an arcane concept. History tells us that the intent of labor and union leaders was to prevent workers from being abused through overwork during the age of industrialization. Nowadays, however, the forty-hour workweek is more of an impediment—and an unhelpful one.

Consider the concept of extra credit. In elementary school when you completed some additional work, you received an extra five points toward your grade. Did we do the extra work because we wanted to better ourselves? Probably not—we just wanted something extra. We have been conditioned to believe that we need an incentive to do something "extra." In reality, all the incentive we should need is knowing we are investing in ourselves and challenging ourselves to go beyond "the standard." Those who go the extra mile find less competition and achieve better outcomes. The fewer people who are willing to go the extra mile, the less "traffic" there is for those of us who are.

RECIPE #64: ACTION AND REACTION

There Is Great Power in Understanding Cause and Effect

What do you want people to say about you at your funeral? Have you ever thought about the impact you'd like to leave on the world? These thought-provoking questions can force you to assess the current status and future trajectory of your life. We have all heard of the Law of Cause and Effect, which states that every action has a reaction. This law is true at the individual level as well: your thoughts, actions, and the way you interact with others will result in other effects that will have an impact on your life.

There is immense power in this universal law because it makes the course of our lives more predictable. For example, if you seek success, there are specific actions and behaviors (causes) that can result in success (effects). However, there is a particular fallacy that pervades modern societies. There is a negative corollary: most humans worry so much about what others will think about our actions that we lose the ability to create the effects we seek. This dynamic has had a staggering impact on our lives because the thoughts and opinions of others can dominate and overwhelm our own behaviors. The point is this: think for yourself and act on your own behalf; the thoughts or actions of others cannot result in any meaningful effects you desire.

RECIPE #65: BEING INTERESTED IS NOT BEING COMMITTED

Writing Down Your Goals Is Not Enough

The 1972 Miami Dolphins are the only NFL football team to go undefeated over an entire season. That team's commitment to winning the Super Bowl—and commitment to each other—is legendary. I've wondered how Don Shula, the Dolphins' coach, motivated his team to succeed in this endeavor. He once said, "I feel you set a goal to be your best and then work every waking hour of each day trying to achieve that goal. The ultimate goal is victory, and if you refuse to work as hard as you possibly can toward that aim, or if you do anything that keeps you from achieving that goal, then you are just cheating yourself."

The lesson here is simple: you are kidding yourself if your desired outcomes are just thoughts or words on paper. Thoughts or words on paper show that you are more "interested" than you are committed—commitment means taking deliberate action to move toward your goals. Without full commitment, your life goals will remain elusive.

RECIPE #66: BE AUTHENTIC

You Can't Earn Trust If You Lack Character

It seems that the importance of character has lost some of its value. Our interactions with one another have become so transactional, one-dimensional, or in many cases, simply "fake." Just think about how people create "avatars" of themselves on social media platforms. What many people broadcast to the world about themselves is not who they really are, it's just a *caricature* of who they want to be perceived as. I see this phenomenon as a symptom of a lack of character, or worse, a discomfort with who we really are, as individuals.

It is interesting that the word *character* (which has Greek origins) literally means "to make a mark." What mark are you making on the world? And what marks are you misrepresenting? This concept translates to our everyday lives as well. I know I personally have been guilty of not bringing my "full self" to the workplace or social situations, because of my fear of being judged. This behavior demonstrated a lack of character on my part, and this is something that I have worked to improve. What I've found is that being more authentic can have extremely positive effects. Why? Because authenticity is the core building block of establishing trust in every relationship.

RECIPE #67: DON'T BE A RUDDERLESS BOAT

Without Direction, You Will End up Nowhere

Imagine if you had the fanciest boat, one with all the bells and whistles—everything except the rudder. A boat's rudder is the instrument used to change direction. Without a rudder, it would not take long for your boat to be lost at sea, or even worse—sink! Our minds are very much the same. How often do you stop and think about the things that are actually important to you?

Countless thought leaders in recent history, from Napoleon Hill to Earl Nightingale to Ralph Waldo Emerson, have articulated that our thoughts create our experiences. In other words, our experiences as humans are often defined by what we are thinking about constantly. This leads me to wonder why so many of us fail to spend time thinking *strategically* about "the what" and "the how" that determine whether we will achieve our goals. For instance, if you spend time thinking about how terrible your day will be tomorrow, guess what...it will be awful. You can purposefully direct your thoughts to focus on what you want your life experience to be, and on the steps you will need to take to get there. This is the importance of strategy. Without doing this, you'll be a ship at sea without a rudder.

RECIPE #68: WE ARE ALL PHONE ADDICTS

Your Progress Killer Is in Your Pocket

I recently watched an interview with Robin Sharma, author of *The Monk Who Sold His Ferrari*. During the interview, Robin made me realize that I was addicted to my phone (and I know most of you reading this have the same addiction). He explained the science behind the addiction and I will do my best to simplify it here.

Have you ever picked up your phone a few times and felt disappointed because there were no new text messages or no "likes" on your most recent Instagram post? Every time we receive a new message or like, our brain supplies us with a shot of a chemical called dopamine, which causes what can be described as a "mini high" and gives us a positive feeling. This is one of the most productivity-killing behaviors there is, and one that practically all of us are guilty of. How much time do you spend glued to your phone every day? Take it from Robin—unplug from your phone for at least an hour per day.

RECIPE #69: THE MOST VALUABLE TRAIT

Resourcefulness Is the Ultimate Resource

Resourcefulness is defined as "the ability to meet situations." That seems simple enough, but its meaning is relevant to both our everyday lives and our ability to achieve. To quote Tony Robbins, "It's not the lack of resources, it's your lack of resourcefulness that causes failure." What should this mean to you? Being resourceful is about nurturing an ability to find quick solutions to complex problems. People who are resourceful do not complain or mull over how something went wrong—instead, they take bold, thoughtful, and immediate action to find ways to deal with hardship (and often turn hardship into opportunity).

The most innovative entrepreneurs in the world are often the most resourceful. They aren't succeeding because they are more intelligent or better than everyone else—they simply understand how to best operate within resource-constrained environments. It's in their DNA to adapt and overcome setbacks. We can all do the same on an individual level by being strategic about how we spend our time and money, making the best out of what we have, and refusing to allow challenges to impede our progress.

RECIPE #70: THE TRUTH ABOUT TRUTH

Optics Can Distort the Truth

I was thirteen when Al Cowlings and O. J. Simpson took the Los Angeles police on the most infamous car chase in American history. At the time, I was too young to understand the complex atmospherics related to race, sports, culture, and justice that were at play that day, and in the trial that followed. Obviously a verdict was determined, but in the "court of public opinion," I believe we had—and still have—a hung jury.

Regardless of what you think of O. J. or the verdict, we know that the "optics" of any situation are important and that optics often influence the beliefs of millions of people. Be careful to consider the optics of your behavior every day, for there will be plenty of people ready to manipulate or capitalize on the opportunity to paint you in a certain light.

RECIPE #71: FAILURE IS A JOURNEY

Life Is a Never-Ending Dance with Failure

You've noticed that embracing failure is a theme in this book. At this point, it might be helpful to reframe what we understand failure to be. Even the very definitions of "failure" have in fact failed us! Failure is defined as a "lack of success or a state of inability to perform a normal function."

The problem with the definition is that people think of failure as being confined to a particular event or specific period of time. This could not be further from the truth. We should perceive the word *failure* in the same way we understand the word *journey*. What do you think about when you hear or read the word *journey*? A journey is a sequence of events that occurs as we move, over time, to a destination or end state. Failure should be understood in the same manner. The act of being unsuccessful at something teaches you that your approach is insufficient. Thus, when trying again, you should recognize that a different approach is needed if you're going to succeed. This determinative cycle of *feedback* is what allows you to zero in on what you need to do to achieve your objectives. Failure is a process—not a momentary event. Learn from it as you go, as you do on a journey.

RECIPE #72: READING IS FUNDAMENTAL

Read at Least Thirty Minutes Per Day

Brace yourself! I am going to divulge the most valuable success secret in the world. And here it is: the more people read, the more successful they are. Of course, there are exceptions, but consider the fact that the average Fortune 500 CEO reads more than fifty books per year. Randall Bell, author of *Me We Do Be: The Four Cornerstones of Success*, conducted a study that surveyed nearly five thousand people of different backgrounds and socioeconomic statuses. He found that those who read seven or more books every year are 122 percent more likely to achieve millionaire status. Let that sink in. Now think about how much you read.

From this day forward, make a commitment to read at least thirty minutes per day. Be sure that some of that reading relates to your field or industry. Most people will not, which means you will have an edge over the masses. Want to take it up a notch? Then read for eight hours a day—that's Warren Buffett's routine!

RECIPE #73:
ETIQUETTE IS KEY

Bad Manners Lead to Even Worse Outcomes

Inappropriate or unprofessional etiquette has destroyed many business deals. There are those who have an amazing command of language, networking ability, and people skills, and who always know how to say the right thing. For the rest of us, unfortunately, we must work harder to understand the unwritten rules that apply to professional settings, social environments, and personal relationships.

Etiquette means that your behavior is acceptable and welcomed in a particular setting. Being late to a business meeting is neither acceptable nor welcomed and reflects poor etiquette. It also demonstrates a lack of respect for the individual you are meeting. This is a critical and complex topic you must master if you are looking to succeed in life. Make it a point to study and practice the proper etiquette for your social and professional environments if you're serious about achieving your goals.

RECIPE #74: EJECT PROPERLY

Quit with Grace

Committing to something, and then deciding to give up because it's "too" challenging, is something I will never understand. Perhaps this is a result of my time in uniform because, in the army, if you set out to do something, you do your best to complete the mission. But in reality, there are some missions that are simply not worth the collateral damage. If your professional circumstance or life pursuit brings you nothing but frustration and heartache, going in a different direction may be warranted. And yes, there are times when it's okay to want to quit a friendship, job, business, relationship, or project if it's clear that the outcome is not worth the effort you are putting in.

In these situations, you will need to weigh the risks and rewards that will result from quitting. If you decide to quit, the most important part is to make sure that you eject properly. Separating on good terms is critically important to your reputation. Offending a supervisor, business partner, or associate by leaving in a "blaze of glory" is the wrong answer. Be honest, be respectful, and separate with grace.

RECIPE #75: THE MOST IMPORTANT FOUR-LETTER WORD

Earn

We can all agree that there is a certain dignity that comes with "earning" things we value. There are a lot of positive emotions associated with earning a result or creating things that other people value through tireless work. Why don't more people do it, then? Thomas Edison once said: "Opportunity is missed by most people because it is dressed in overalls and looks like work." This quote captures the essence of where we are today when there has never been as much of an obsession with instant gratification.

The principle of *earning* is essentially about one thing—*work*. Creating wealth or accumulating more money is only one dimension of what it means to *earn*. If you want to be a better person, nurture more productive relationships, or become healthier, you must earn it by committing to behaviors that are consistent with your desired outcome. The reward for "earning behaviors" is the progress or value that you receive by taking the necessary actions to achieve your goals. Go to work and start *earning* outcomes.

RECIPE #76: SELF-DISCIPLINE VERSUS SELF-CONTROL

Understand the Difference—You Need Both

I once struggled to understand the difference between self-discipline and self-control, but I know now that they are actually very different, and the difference between them is important. Self-discipline is forward-looking—it is the power you use to keep doing a particular thing even though you don't feel like it. For example, getting up and going to the gym five days per week requires self-discipline. Self-control, on the other hand, is the power to say no or to stop a specific behavior. For example, if you are having a few drinks with friends but you must drive home, self-control is what happens when you cut yourself off so you can get home safely.

To accomplish your goals, you need both self-discipline and self-control. You can have all the self-discipline in the world in the form of establishing goals, sticking to a routine, and sustaining behaviors that will drive progress. However, lacking self-control along the way increases the probability of self-sabotage that can derail your journey. To achieve your desired outcomes, embrace and practice both.

RECIPE #77: DEVELOP A GROWTH MINDSET

It Doesn't Pay to Be a Know-It-All

We all know the type of people who take up all the oxygen in the room—the folks with the biggest ideas and best stories—those who talk a lot more than they listen. I have the right to talk about these types of people because I was once on the path to becoming one of them. A characteristic of these types—the know-it-alls—is that they would rather talk about what they know than learn the things they don't.

Research (see Carol Dweck's book *Mindset: The New Psychology of Success*) shows that some people maintain a *fixed mindset* and find it important to "show off" their knowledge, skills, and abilities; other people have a *growth mindset* and understand the value of continuous learning and development. Individuals with a growth mindset have a "toolbox" full of content and experience—they are better prepared to react when confronted with both challenges and opportunities. Never forget: people who learn more, earn more! Grow your mindset.

RECIPE #78: CONSEQUENCES HAVE CONSEQUENCES

Play The "Long Game"

The idea of the "long game" instructs us to employ a disciplined, long-term strategy to accomplish our goals. However, our preoccupation with social media and instant gratification has driven "impulsive thinking" to become the norm rather than the exception. Impulsive thinkers are short-sighted—they lack the desire or will to consider all of the consequences of their actions and ideas. Often, this behavior leads to unintended problems because they "leapt before they looked."

Disciplined (or critical) thinkers have a very different approach. They thoughtfully consider the initial, secondary, and tertiary consequences that will result if they take a specific action. They know that every action has primary consequences, and there will *also* be a trailing set of additional consequences they will need to confront. The lesson here is do not play the "short game." Think long-term.

RECIPE #79: DECLARE WAR ON MEDIOCRITY

*Challenge Yourself to Step Out
of the "Average" Crowd*

The authenticity and grittiness of David Goggins's memoir, *Can't Hurt Me*, reminded me of aspects of my own upbringing. He underscores that it should be your goal to be "uncommon amongst uncommon people." It can be very easy to associate with people who will not challenge you, those who will let you get away with shortcuts, or who are satisfied with the "status quo." Too easy.

Such people—the mediocre type—will have little positive influence on your life, and you will do well to stay away from them as much as you can. Why? Because mediocrity spreads like a virus! The cure, if you catch the virus, is to work your ass off and challenge yourself to do better every single day. The work will be hard, but you can take comfort in knowing that when you commit yourself to the sacrifice that comes with a determination to achieve a goal, you will differentiate yourself from those who are willing to live with mediocrity. The mediocre folks will still be comfortable in the same place you left them.

RECIPE #80: BREAKING OUT OF THE BOX

Stop Limiting Your Beliefs

"Thinking outside of the box" is an overused cliché, but it maintains its appeal in workplaces every day. I have challenged others with their use of this phrase on many occasions. The point of the phrase is to encourage people to question the limits of what is possible, but I've come to realize that believing in limitations has become easy for all of us. Our minds accept limitations because they're comfortable, but this is not the relationship we should have with limits.

We should more instinctively perceive any limit as an invitation to create a solution or an alternative approach. What I'm saying is that thinking outside of the box shouldn't be seen as revolutionary—it should be the norm. The innovators who are touted for "breaking out of the box" are no different than you. Whatever limiting beliefs you have—break out of them. Your "box" is mere fiction.

RECIPE #81: MAINTAIN THE RIGHT ATTITUDE ABOUT MONEY

Money Is Not the "Root of All Evil"

While I do not agree with all of Robert Kiyosaki's views—some of which are controversial—he has given the world an important financial lesson that has nothing to do with money. One of the themes of his *Rich Dad, Poor Dad* franchise is that acquiring wealth has a lot to do with your attitude toward money. When you were growing up, were you told that "money does not grow on trees?" And surely someone else told you that money is the "root of all evil," correct? Altogether, these ideas and expressions create an unhealthy orientation toward money. Part of what we're taught is focused on scarcity and the fear that we will never have the money we need, and part of it conveys a negative attitude about abundance.

To compound the problem, our school systems do not teach our children anything about assets, debt, saving, or cash flow. We're taught that the normal pathway is to go to college, get a job, and live happily within the confines of the "system," but nothing is taught regarding how we should feel *about* money. No wonder we're often confused by economics. But I can tell you this: making money or creating wealth is not evil—it provides a mechanism upon which you can do good for your family, community, and all of humanity. Make as much as you desire so you can help as many people as you can.

RECIPE #82: SACRIFICE OR REGRET

*Do You Prefer the Pain of Sacrifice
or the Agony of Regret?*

Let's face it—sacrifice costs focus, effort, and discipline, and most times it hurts. I loathe waking up at 5:02 a.m., but I do it because I don't want to be consumed by the guilt that I know I'll experience if I sleep in until 7:00 a.m. and lose two hours of productivity. If I did this for seven days straight, I'd give up fourteen hours of work—and give this time to the others who got up and went after their goals. The sense of regret would hurt me a lot more than the few minutes of discomfort I experience between 5:00 and 5:10 a.m.

There is an exercise that I'd like you to try right now. Take ten minutes to think hard about the regret you will feel if you do not get the next promotion, launch your business, or achieve a goal you've made. Afterward, think about the sacrifice and actions you know it will take to get there. Which path do you choose—the one with the sacrifice or the one with the regret? I assure you that the sacrifice to make progress toward your goal is temporary, but the regret from failing to launch will last a lifetime. Go to work.

RECIPE #83: THE ENEMY OF PROGRESS

Procrastination Should Not Be Comfortable

According to a University of Cambridge study, procrastination affects approximately 20 percent of adults and 50 percent of college students (I suspect these numbers are really much higher). It's easy to delay actions or decisions that you know you need to make, even if the indecision runs counter to your best interests. It surely comes at a grave cost. The real price of procrastination is lack of *progress*.

Procrastination negates progress, and anything that stands in the way of progress is your enemy. Take steps to make procrastination uncomfortable. When I recognize I'm procrastinating, I call myself out directly with some very derogatory self-talk. For example, I might say, "Get up, you piece of shit; the project is not going to finish itself." For some reason, this motivates me to move. This same tactic might not be right for you; however, you should challenge yourself to figure out an approach that minimizes your acceptance of procrastination.

RECIPE #84: IT'S NOT LONELY AT THE TOP

There Is No Such Thing as Being "Self-Made"

For generations, we've been told that it's "lonely at the top." What that's supposed to mean is that after an individual achieves the highest levels of success, there are fewer people for them to have meaningful relationships with. But is that true? Human nature reveals that rewarding individuals and teams for their accomplishments through recognition and praise is critically important to organizational success.

High-performance individuals in business, sports, and philanthropy are masters at expressing recognition and praise. They are self-aware enough to acknowledge that their success is connected with the triumphs of other people. Do you think Tom Brady could have become Tom Brady without the rest of the players on the Patriots' (or Buccaneers') Super Bowl teams? When you reach the top, you'll find that you're surrounded by plenty of people—the ones who helped you get there.

RECIPE #85: CAPITALISM DRIVES VALUE

*Capitalism Rewards People Who
Bring Value to the Masses*

Capitalism is sometimes met with a tremendous amount of scrutiny and contempt. It's almost as if an idea that improves the lives of millions upon millions of people is a bad thing. If you disagree, then why are the ultrarich often villainized for their wealth? "Those filthy billionaires are just greedy and want to keep everything for themselves." This perspective is grossly inaccurate.

Charles and David Koch have been depicted in the media as billionaire political donors willing to do anything to influence elections. Did you know that the companies they've built make things that you probably use every single day—from toilet paper to electronics? More importantly for me, they make combat uniforms for America's military branches. Their products bring value to many hundreds of millions of people every day. And yes, our economic system rewards them dearly for it—as it should. Capitalism, despite some of its shortcomings, raises the standard of living for everyone.

RECIPE #86: TURN YOUR CHALLENGES UPSIDE DOWN

Solve Problems Backward

Charlie Munger is one of the richest Americans people have never heard of. His investment prowess is second to none—he helped build Berkshire Hathaway into a multibillion-dollar conglomerate along with Warren Buffett. I am fascinated by his concept of "inversion." This idea focuses on looking at problems in reverse or attempting to solve them "backward." For example, my daughter plays competitive tennis, and her coach routinely encourages her to focus on not losing rather than working so hard to win. Instead of being hyper aggressive, the inversion approach allows her to stick to the basics and keep the ball in play until, eventually, her opponent makes a mistake.

Going forward, try to look at your challenges from an inverse perspective. It might force you to consider everything you should *not* do to drive an outcome, which in many cases is more valuable than focusing on the few things you *should* do to achieve your objective.

RECIPE #87: BE PART OF A COMMUNITY

Serve Causes Bigger than Yourself

What did you post on TikTok, Instagram, or Twitter today? If nothing, that's fantastic—it probably means you were too busy being productive. For those of you who did have time to post, I am willing to bet that your contribution to the world was probably about *you*. There's nothing wrong with this in moderation, but the fact is that most people are too preoccupied with themselves. By and large, it seems that we have lost the value of service and the appeal of enriching the communities and the environments around us.

When was the last time you donated your time to a cause that you are passionate about—one that would not result in a tangible benefit to you? Giving back to our communities is critically important. There are intangible benefits such as creating new friendships, improving your psychological well-being, and debunking misperceptions you might have about people you don't interact with under normal circumstances. Take a step and find a place to volunteer your time. Contribute to a community initiative that will bring joy, comfort, or satisfaction to others. You will thank yourself for doing so. And if you must post pictures of yourself, post images of you serving your community.

RECIPE #88: A VISUAL MIND MATTERS

Leverage the Power of Visualization

Did you ever wake up terrified in the middle of the night because of a bad dream? The brain can play cruel tricks on us—it can lead us to believe that the monsters that were chasing us in the dream were real and will eventually catch us and rip us to shreds. Good thing for us, we can use this condition to our advantage.

Visualization is one of the most powerful tools available to us. Athletes, innovators, and high-performance individuals have used visualization techniques for years. Science confirms that in many cases, our brains emit the same neural activity when we are *envisioning* doing something as when we are *actually* doing the same activity in real life. These techniques are effective because your subconscious mind takes cues from your conscious mind without you knowing it. The key here is to be intentional about visualizing your goals and how you will feel when you achieve them. When you do that enough times, your brain will ensure that your actions and behaviors are in alignment with your objectives.

RECIPE #89: DO THINGS THAT SUCK

Confronting Hard Things Will Change Your Life

Can you imagine writing a book report during summer vacation in Las Vegas? That's what happened to me in the summer of 1994. I spent that summer with my father, who lived in Las Vegas at the time. For the most part, I had a blast, but one particular day will forever live in infamy in my mind. I had done something to make him angry (what it was, I honestly do not remember), and my punishment was to read a book and handwrite a five-page book report. I wasn't allowed to do anything else until it was complete; I was beyond furious, but I did it. The book was *Makes Me Wanna Holler* by Nathan McCall, and I remember that it was 448 pages long.

Looking back, I see that it was a defining moment in my life because after I was done, I felt a deep sense of accomplishment—and I wanted to read more. It turned me into a lifelong student and voracious reader. Doing something that totally sucked changed my life in a positive way...forever. There is probably something that "sucks" that you know will make you a better person. Do more of it starting today.

RECIPE #90: THE CIRCLE OF SAFETY

Create Space for People to Thrive

Simon Sinek's *Leaders Eat Last* resonated with me because it uses military examples to illuminate essential leadership behaviors. I found the book's message so important that I decided to give a copy to fifty engineering leaders who came together for a technology summit in 2022.

One of the book's core messages centers on the idea of establishing a "Circle of Safety" among teams. Within the Circle of Safety, team members are allowed to operate "freely," where diversity of thought is encouraged and making mistakes is not met with criticism. Each team's leader is responsible for protecting both the people as well as the environment created within the circle. Ensure that you create such a circle of safety within your family, workplace, team, or organization. Safety is one of the key elements needed to drive high-performance teams (and families) to achieve shared objectives.

RECIPE #91:
STAY HUNGRY

Live Every Day as If You Are Starving

Complacency is extremely dangerous. Another of those behaviors that is an enemy of progress, I think it's even more sinister than procrastination. Being complacent means having a sense of self-satisfaction or being pleased with oneself, even in the face of danger or perilous consequences. The kind of people who live with complacency are the same type who are happy to be part of the "status quo." They rarely challenge themselves to go the extra mile. Why go the extra mile when you have already reached a comfortable plateau? Never let yourself feel this way.

Starting today, banish your mind's ability to feel like you have arrived at your goal, and replace it with an insatiable hunger for more. If you reached a goal without a struggle, that probably means the outcome was too easy. No matter how successful you are, there will always be people who continue to push the limits of achievement, and they may enjoy higher levels of success. Try to be one of these achievers—the people who are not comfortably sitting on their plateau. If you allow yourself to become complacent, you've already begun a steady decline. The slow burn of unjustified self-satisfaction will consume your ability to achieve meaningful outcomes over time.

RECIPE #92: LIVE ABUNDANTLY

Take Control of Your Own Abundance

Some people think of "living abundantly" as negative or gluttonous. But for me, it's about enhancing one's quality of life. *Abundance* is not simply about money or acquiring material things. It is more of a mindset you adopt that allows you to embrace your potential to achieve aspirational outcomes. It is about moving beyond anything you may have perceived as your "limitations."

You should never accept your "limitations," even subconsciously, because that will result in a feeling of scarcity—a feeling that you will never live as abundantly as you want to. The first step is to define what abundance means to you. Does it mean love, health, success, wealth, or service? Maybe something else? Our lives are filled with endless opportunities and infinite possibilities. The people who are deliberate about planning, setting goals, and committing to the work of which they are capable are also the ones who will discover (and maintain) abundance.

RECIPE #93: LEARNING THROUGH LOSING

Adversity Reveals Who We Really Are

I *hate* to lose. As a result, I think often about the current generation and the way we are training children to run from adversity instead of through it. We are teaching them that second place is okay—and it's not. This approach can have devastating effects on the psyche of a child.

I am not saying that there is a problem with not coming in first—someone has to come in second! However, we should be teaching our youth that being second means being the first person to lose (stop giving out "participation" trophies). We should be instilling the idea that coming in second means that they need to train harder, study more, and apply more rigor to their craft, so the next time they compete, coming in first may be achievable. People who decide to go over, under, or through adversity are happier, more successful, and more emotionally resilient. Become this type of person.

RECIPE #94: WHAT ARE YOU WAITING FOR?

A Single Idea Can Be Revolutionary

Take one minute to study the environment around you. Within your reach, there is probably an iPhone, laptop, and other gadgets. You are most likely sitting in some form of comfortable chair, sofa, or lounge furniture. And lastly, you may have a Starbucks latte sitting next to you, or perhaps you had one this morning before you hopped into an Uber or a Tesla to begin your day.

My point is that companies like Apple, Ikea, Starbucks, Uber, and Tesla have revolutionized consumer behavior on a grand scale. The common denominator they share is that these products and businesses started with a single idea that focused on transforming people's daily lives. Most big ideas like these fail, but that should not dissuade you from working as hard as you can to bring your own ideas to life. Do you have an idea that you've been kicking around in your head for years? What has stopped you from creating a plan to pursue it? Put your idea on paper and just *go*. Getting started is half the battle.

RECIPE #95: EXCUSES ARE A DISEASE

Vaccinate Yourself against Excuses

Not everything goes according to plan—we all know this. Yet when something goes wrong, spending our energy wallowing in excuses is a terrible use of time. I hear this theme every time I tune into the *Joe Rogan Experience* podcast. Sometimes excuses are true, but they do *not* give you the right to turn your future over to them. Benjamin Franklin once said, "He that is good for making excuses is seldom good for anything else." Well said from my perspective.

Excuses can be likened to a disease because, if left unchecked, they can spread across many areas of your life. They give us an "out," when we know deep down we've decided not to face an uncomfortable situation or failed to meet a standard we hold ourselves to. Luckily, there is a defense for the disease, and you can immunize yourself against it. Examine why you are making an excuse. Did you put undue pressure on yourself because of an unrealistic deadline? Are your expectations achievable? Can you recover from setbacks and keep moving toward your goals? Excuses are like speed bumps...slow down, drive over them, and then accelerate.

RECIPE #96: TRIVIAL THINKING LEADS TO TRIVIAL OUTCOMES

"Don't Major in Minor Things"

You become what you think about. We've heard this from countless authors and thought leaders in one form or another. Entrepreneur Jim Rohn captured this idea when he said, "Don't major in minor things." Think about the amount of time you waste contemplating things that have little impact on your life.

We are all guilty of being caught up in trivial things that rarely lead to desirable outcomes. It is noteworthy that the word *trivial* originates from the Latin word *trivialis*, which means "appropriate to the street corner, commonplace, or vulgar." But big thinking and innovative ideas are anything but common. Furthermore, I am not sure if having thoughts that are "appropriate to the street corner" is going to help you accomplish things that are important to you. Focus your thoughts on the things you need to do to experience the life you envision for yourself.

RECIPE #97: P.I.E.

Always Work Your P.I.E.

The current chief information officer of Northrop Grumman, a US-based manufacturer of advanced weapon systems and aerial platforms, is a great mentor and someone I consider to be one of my best friends.

In 2009, he introduced me to the P.I.E. concept, which has literally changed my life. The acronym stands for *Preparation, Influence, and Exposure*—three words that have defined my career and facilitated my journey to grow in a number of areas. If you embrace each of these three concepts, there is nothing you will not be able to achieve in a corporate-based career. Here are the principles:

1. **Preparation:** be prepared to take on your manager's duties as well as the responsibilities of your manager's manager.
2. **Influence:** earn credibility by demonstrating visible impact across your organization. Deliver discernible results.
3. **Exposure:** be deliberate about volunteering for tough challenges and embrace every opportunity to show your value to those who have the power to make decisions.

RECIPE #98: WHAT MOTIVATES YOU?

Motivation Is Not the Cause of Action; It's the By-Product of It

Motivation is a complicated term and one that is often misunderstood. How many times have you told yourself that you have to get motivated so you can accomplish a specific task? This is *not* how motivation actually works. Motivation is created by taking an action for which you will be rewarded once it is completed. There are two types of motivation: extrinsic motivation and intrinsic motivation. Extrinsic motivation is based on your desire to receive an external reward, such as money or other material things. Intrinsic motivation is very different—it is about the internal satisfaction we experience when we do what we said we were going to do.

Typically, the most successful people are intrinsically motivated because they are not dependent on others or external rewards. Their behavior is not influenced by outside forces. Furthermore, this type of motivation is more sustainable because you are less focused on short-term incentives and more focused on broader goals. Get clear on what motivates you internally instead of being driven by external rewards. The more you turn inside yourself to find inspiration, the more your personal motivation will increase.

RECIPE #99: HONOR WHAT YOU VALUE

Value Determines Discipline

The importance of staying disciplined has been explored throughout this book. The benefits of discipline are so clear that it leads us to wonder: why would anyone choose lack of discipline? The answer is simple: we choose lack of discipline because we gain more value or pleasure from undisciplined behavior than we do from disciplined behavior.

I get it—staying disciplined is hard, and not always "fun." But if you think about it, you will see the value of sticking to your commitments. For example, if you love doughnuts but you also want to lose twenty pounds, you must convince yourself that the value of losing weight is greater than the value of the taste of fried dough drenched in powdered sugar. If you don't see it that way, it means you do not truly value your stated goal of losing weight. It also indicates that, until you change, you will always be a slave to your impulses. Be honest with yourself about what you value and ensure that your behaviors are consistent with the outcomes you deem important.

RECIPE #100: A HEALTHY DIET FOR THE MIND

Feed Your Brain with the Right Nourishment

By now, I hope you have a better appreciation for how your mindset shapes your perspectives, habits, and behaviors. These Recipes were intended to be a healthy "diet" regimen for your mind, coming at a moment in history where we waste so much time every day. According to *Smart Insights*, there are close to five billion people worldwide who use social media. Users spend an average of nearly two and a half hours per day on these platforms. We humans spend approximately twelve billion hours per day on Facebook, Instagram, TikTok, Telegram, and other social media services. Wow! Can you imagine if we harnessed that time and brainpower and focused it on solving the world's problems?

Those who choose to spend their time learning and developing themselves will ultimately achieve more success, wealth, happiness, and self-actualization because they've committed to becoming more productive people. Be one of those individuals...do not let your brain continuously gain useless "weight," which will prevent you from achieving your desired outcomes. If you do, it will end up "weighing" a metaphorical *500 pounds*...

CONCLUSION

Thank you for going on this journey. I recognize that parts of this book might not be applicable to you—the relevance of these principles depends on each person's own life situation. I have made so many mistakes in life; nevertheless, I am thankful for all of them. My mission has been to describe the mindset-changing lessons that were important to me, with the belief that they might be able to help you on your journey too. It is my hope that at least a few of the Recipes will lead you to life changes that will propel you to reach your goals.

There are ten key ideas I'd like you to keep in mind:

1. Ambition is *good*.
2. Don't just set goals—be *obsessed* with them.
3. *Discipline* is the foundation of achievement.
4. Always *outwork* your peers and competition.
5. Procrastination *derails* progress.
6. Ignore social *sabotage*—who cares what others think?
7. *Think* deliberately and control your emotions.
8. Choose your social circles *wisely*.
9. *Learn* like your life depends on it.
10. *Serve* as many people as you can.

So what is next for you? As I have said over and over in this book, changing your perspectives and mindset is the key to changing your life. To achieve your goals and the outcomes you're reaching for, you have to become the person who is capable of attaining those goals and outcomes, and that means changing your behaviors. Again, your brain is just like a body. You must bring in the right mental nutrients so your mind can function in its most optimal state. Commit to adopting behaviors that contribute to progress and make yourself accountable.

If you follow just a quarter of the lessons in this book, you will become a different person. Reward yourself as you work every day to move closer to your desired outcomes because every victory matters. This book is designed to set a standard in matters of mindset, and I have incorporated lessons from many of the greatest minds in history and distilled them to help you recalibrate your own. It is up to you to decide, plan, commit, and take immediate action. The person you are destined to become is waiting for you.

Lastly, I would like to make one humble request. I am on a mission to change the mindset of one billion people through the *500 Pound* book series, *500 Pound Academy*, and *500 Pound* podcast. I know—it's an audacious goal but that is what being a visionary requires—setting out to achieve what many consider impossible. Please share a copy of this book with the five people you care about most to help me in this endeavor. There are a lot of 500-pound brains out there, and I am making it my life's work to put them on the right mental "diet."

I would also love to hear your story as you make progress toward your goals. I can be reached at info@500poundmedia. com. You can also find valuable insights and content at www. 500poundmedia.com.

Time to Go to Work,
Derrick

ACKNOWLEDGMENTS

I owe a humble thank-you to the many people who have shared their wisdom with the world and with me personally—I could not have written this book without them. From the posthumous souls listed here to those who are still with us, I thank you all. I am forever indebted to each and every one of you: John Russell, Priscilla Lott-Price, Gerry Fasano, Jim Carlini, Doug Jones, Robert Franceschini, Roger Krone, JD Kathuria, Sid Fuchs, Curtis "50 Cent" Jackson, Marc Gerald, David Goggins, Oprah, Barbara Corcoran, Jocko Willink, Dwayne "The Rock" Johnson, Will Smith, Sara Blakely, Andy Frisella, Napoleon Hill, Ed Mylett, Robert Greene, Gary Vaynerchuk, Jeff Bezos, Barack and Michelle Obama, Warren Buffett, Angela Duckworth, Elon Musk, Kobe Bryant, Steve Jobs, Dr. Randall Bell, Nelson Mandela, Earl Nightingale, Mel Robbins, Jim Rohn, Tony Robbins, Robert Kiyosaki, James Clear, Michael Dell, Joe Rogan, Michael Jordan, Steve Harvey, Tyler Perry, Stephen Covey, Jay-Z, Grant Cardone, Patrick Bet-David, Brian Tracy, Robert F. Smith, Robin Sharma, Dr. Sylvia Boorstein, Eric Thomas, Serena Williams, Jordan Peterson, Tom Brady, Ralph Waldo Emerson, Alex Hormozi, Bob Proctor, Denzel Washington, Malcolm Gladwell, Matthew McConaughey, Jack Welch, Charlie Munger, Daymond John, Kim Kardashian, Jon Maxwell, Mark Cuban, Les Brown, Dan Peña, Dr. Wayne Dyer, Daniel Goleman, Aubrey "Drake" Graham, Tom Bilyeu, Bedros Keuilian, Darren Hardy, Admiral William McRaven, Thomas Edison, Arnold Schwarzenegger, Spencer Johnson, Neil Pasricha, Floyd Mayweather, Dean

Graziosi, Ramit Sethi, Alexandra Cooper, Robert Cialdini, Oscar Wilde, Sylvester Stallone, Dr. Carol Dweck, Aliko Dangote, Ray Dalio, Sheryl Sandberg, Richard Branson, Brené Brown, Simon Sinek, Jim Collins, John Wooden, Tom Newberry, Blake Shelton, Dale Carnegie, David Allen, Nathan McCall, and countless other influences.

To my close friends and family, the greatest gift of my life is that all of you continue to believe in me. That means everything.

To my Scribe Media family who helped me bring this book to reality, thank you for your candor, patience, vision, and continued support (Chip Blake, Ryan Garcia, Miles Rote, Annette Mims, Kathy Shady, Sophie May, and countless others behind the scenes). This team is the epitome of "world-class."

Printed in Great Britain
by Amazon

46752209R00128